INSANE SPEED

STOCK CAR MANIA

by Craig Stevens

A Crabtree Seedlings Book

CRABTREE
Publishing Company
www.crabtreebooks.com

RAGÚ
Nationwide
7
RAGÚ
GOODYEAR
MOOG
MAHLE
COMP
DISCOUNT
tires.com
TIRE
PENNZOIL
Ford
MUSTANG
22
Nationwide
GOODYEAR
MAHLE
MOOG

Table of Contents

STOCK CAR MANIA

Race car drivers are brave.

They drive cars
really fast.

Nationwide
RAGU
GOODYEAR
Holley
3M
Edelbrock
SIMPSON
MOOG
MAHLE
COMP
SUNOCO

Stock cars are built to go fast.

KAULIG RACING
SIMPSON
RR-3
EAGLE
GOODYEAR

They have special tires.

They have **spoilers** that change how air flows around the car.

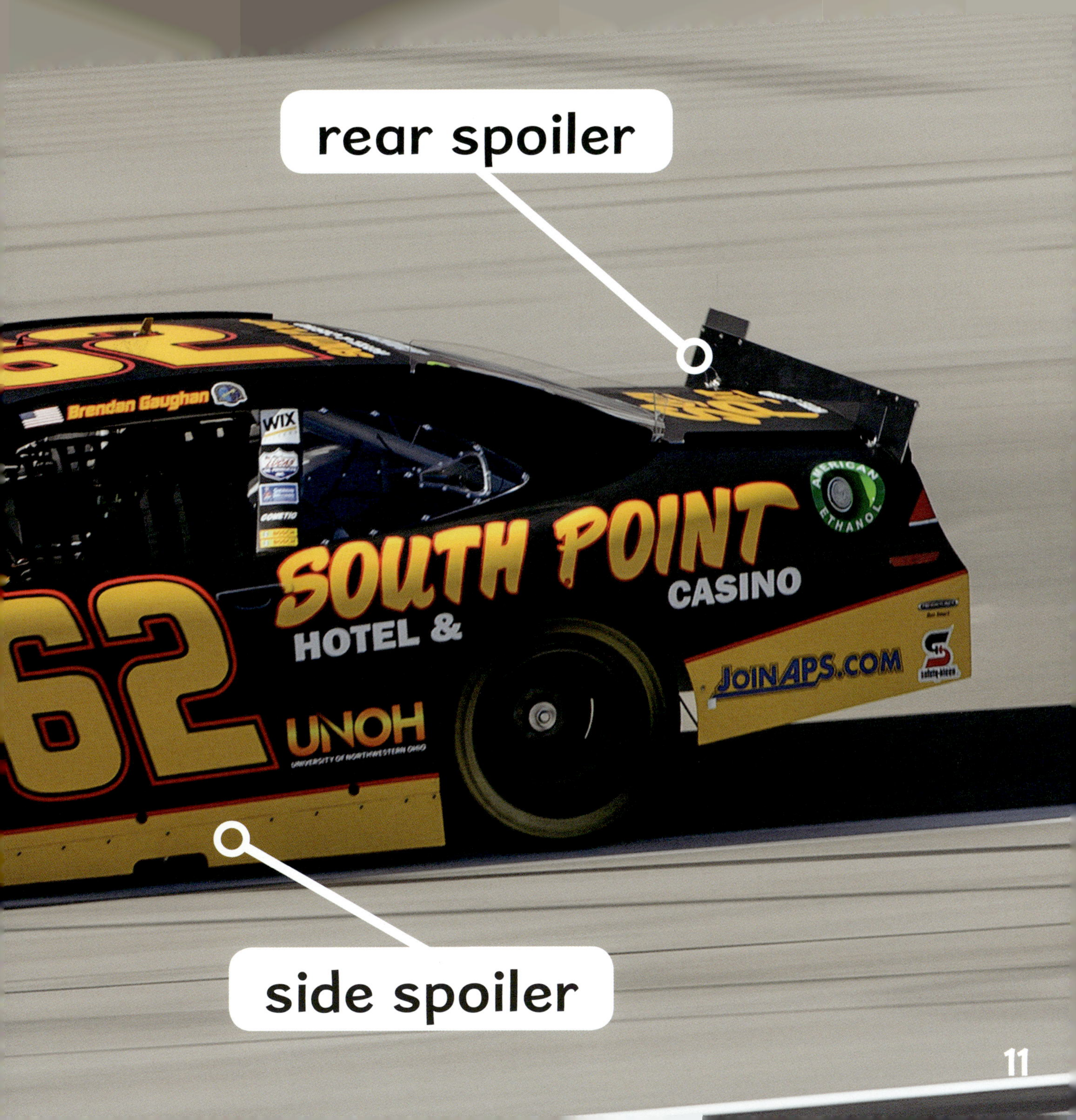
rear spoiler
side spoiler
62
Brendan Gaughan
WIX
SOUTH POINT
HOTEL &
CASINO
UNOH
UNIVERSITY OF NORTHWESTERN OHIO
AMERICAN ETHANOL
JoinAPS.COM

Stock cars have only one seat.

Bass Pro Shops
TRACKER boats
TRACKER boats
McMurray

ADVOCARE
Nationwide Insurance
Zest
Ford
GOODYEAR
SUNOCO
3M
innovation
FASTENAL
TREVOR BAYNE
STENHOUSE JR.

Drivers wear special **gear** to stay safe.

CARFAX

The driver's **pit crew** wears safety gear too.

16
Con·way
GOODYEAR
3M
MSD
FEATHERLITE
PENSKE
Coach-Net
Auto Meter
JEGS
K&N
ARP
MAC TOOLS
Dupli-Color
WIX

Sometimes stock cars crash.

Stock cars race around a track until someone wins.

BRISTOL MOTOR SPEEDWAY
FOOD CITY
O'Reilly AUTO PARTS
SUNOCO
FOOD CITY
OD CITY
R SPEEDWAY

Glossary

gear (GIHR): Gear is equipment or clothing needed to do a job or play a sport.

pit crew (PIT KROO): A pit crew is a team of people that check the race cars and help the drivers during a race.

spoilers (SPOIL-urz): Spoilers change the flow of air around the car to help it stay on the ground and move faster.

stock cars (STOK KARZ): Stock cars are regular cars that have been changed into race cars.

Index

RACE FLAGS

Start the Race

Caution or Slow

Pull into Pit

Stop

Move Over

Last Lap

Race is Finished

School-to-Home Support for Caregivers and Teachers

This book helps children grow by letting them practice reading. Here are a few guiding questions to help the reader build his or her comprehension skills. Possible answers appear here in red.

Before Reading

- **What do I think this book is about?** I think this book is about very fast stock cars. I think this book is about stock car racing.
- **What do I want to learn about this topic?** I want to learn more about the drivers of stock cars. I want to learn what makes a car a stock car.

During Reading

- **I wonder why...** I wonder why stock cars only have one seat. I wonder why stock cars have special tires.
- **What have I learned so far?** I have learned that drivers wear special gear to keep them safe. I have learned that the pit crew team also wears safety gear.

After Reading

- **What details did I learn about this topic?** I have learned that stock cars have spoilers that change how air flows around the car. I have learned that the checkered flag means the race is finished.
- **Read the book again and look for the glossary words.** I see the words *stock cars* on page 7, and the word *spoilers* on page 10. The other glossary words are found on page 22.

Library and Archives Canada Cataloguing in Publication

CIP available at Library and Archives Canada

Library of Congress Cataloging-in-Publication Data

CIP available at Library of Congress

Crabtree Publishing Company
www.crabtreebooks.com 1–800–387–7650

Print book version produced jointly with Blue Door Education in 2022

Written by: Craig Stevens

Print coordinator: Katherine Berti

Printed in the U.S.A./CG20210915/012022

PHOTO CREDITS:
istock.com, shutterstock.com, COVER: © Andre Ricardo | Dreamstime.com; Pages 2-3, 6-7, 12-13, 14,15, 16-17, 18-19, 20-21, 22: Grindstone Media Group-shutterstock.com; Pages 4, 8-9, 10-11, 22: Action Sports Photography-shutterstock.com; Page 5: Jaggat Rashidi-shutterstock.com; Page 22: Photo Works-shutterstock.com; Page 23: Eyematrix-shutterstock.com

Published in the United States
Crabtree Publishing
347 Fifth Ave.
Suite 1402-145
New York, NY 10016

Published in Canada
Crabtree Publishing
616 Welland Ave.
St. Catharines, Ontario
L2M 5V6